First St**eps out**

...ing a lot more money or time than yo...
... o on gambling?

... he money you've lost in the belief that ...
...tely will win, if only you gamble just
... bit more?

... is book will help you to understand
...ctical things you can do to change your
...aviour;
• ... to set realistic goals and stick to them;
• ... to provide support to a compulsive gambler.

Thi... ook is full of help and answers for you. It will
giv... ou what you need to take the first steps out of
pr... m gambling.

...ow L
...ies, (
...s for

Dedicated to the Memory of
Stephen Butcher and Don Ford

First Steps out of Problem Gambling

Joanna Hughes and
Lisa Ustok

LION

This edition copyright © 2011 Lion Hudson

The authors assert the moral right
to be identified as the authors of this work

A Lion Book
an imprint of
Lion Hudson plc
Wilkinson House, Jordan Hill Road,
Oxford OX2 8DR, England
www.lionhudson.com
ISBN 978 0 7459 5537 7

Distributed by:
UK: Marston Book Services, PO Box 269, Abingdon, Oxon OX14 4YN
USA: Trafalgar Square Publishing, 814 N. Franklin Street, Chicago,
IL 60610
USA Christian Market: Kregel Publications, PO Box 2607, Grand Rapids,
MI 49501

First edition 2011
10 9 8 7 6 5 4 3 2 1 0

A catalogue record for this book is available
from the British Library

Typeset in 10.5/14 ITC Stone Serif
Printed and bound in Malta

Contents

Introduction

Welcome! You are at the beginning of a new journey and by opening this book you are inviting hope into your life. This book tells the story of gambling: how and why we gamble, and what we can do about it. If you want to stop gambling, you need to take stock, listen to yourself, and create a new future in which you are not enslaved by addiction. This book is our way of bringing you our insights that have helped others overcome a gambling problem. It is the path of freedom and hope. We believe that stepping out of gambling will enable you to walk along new paths – paths of emerging joy and satisfaction – leaving behind old, unhelpful patterns of thought and behaviour.

Who is this book for?

This book is for anyone who thinks or even vaguely suspects that they are gambling more than they want to. This feeling may be a desire to stop completely or just reduce your gambling. This book is also for partners or loved ones who are worried about someone's gambling behaviour.

Food for thought

According to a recent study, 68 per cent of adults in the UK had participated in some type of gambling over the previous year. However, gambling can be addictive and the rate of problem gambling in the adult population is around 0.6 per cent. This may not sound much, but it amounts to around 284,000 people.

Why listen to us?

We have extensive history of working with people with addictive behaviours. In the course of our work we have come to realize that there is little help and support for people whose addiction is gambling.

We are passionate about seeing people change. We know that people can and do change; people do walk away from addiction. Walking away from addiction will take a lot of hard work and motivation. If you are desperate to see things change in your life, then this book will help you on your way.

How to use this book

Our advice would be to read through the book from start to finish, using the exercises on the way. After that, the book is designed to be dipped into as a manual or workbook.

Beginning your journey: How are you feeling?

You may be feeling fearful about taking the first step on the path to change. Fear is common when entering a new part of your journey, so write down how you are truly feeling right now. It is important to properly acknowledge to yourself how you are feeling, and to give yourself permission to feel that way, but then to say to yourself that you are still going to have the courage to move forward with your life and see good changes soon.

When you acknowledge a feeling, fear, craving, or desire, either by speaking it out loud or writing it down, by bringing it out into the open you can take away its power and hold over you.

Take a deep breath; take action despite all that is against you. Gambling has stolen from you. It is now time to fight back, take a stand, and reclaim your life and all that it has to offer.

Mythbuster

Some people are born with addictive personalities that they can do nothing about or have any control over.

We are all a mixture of nature and nurture, and everyone has the capacity to change, given the right motivation and help.

1

Gambling problems in focus

Gambling is a popular form of entertainment and an exciting, thrilling form of risk-taking. For these reasons it can also be addictive. There are many places one can gamble legally, ranging from playing poker at a friend's house to casinos in Las Vegas. There are fruit machines in pubs, online betting, bingo, lottery tickets, and scratch cards. Nearly all gambling is available remotely – through the internet or digital television or telephone.

According to newspaper reports and online information, gambling addiction is the fastest-growing addiction problem in the UK (see, for example, www.actiononaddiction.org.uk). Like any other addiction, it can be tackled effectively through treatment and rehabilitation, which is where this "First Steps" book comes in.

When gambling becomes a problem
A distinction is often made between "social gamblers" and "problem gamblers".

Many people gamble, and do so as a pastime with no adverse effects on the rest of their lives. These would be called social gamblers. They would consider gambling to be a form of entertainment and would see the cost of the gambling activity to be payment for the entertainment experienced. Social gamblers would feel in complete control of how much time and money they spend gambling, and if they want to stop, they are able to do so.

Problem gambling, however, involves a certain loss of control. Problem gamblers continue to gamble even if they are experiencing negative consequences as a result of their gambling habit.

If you feel that gambling has become a problem, then there are many people who are in the same position as you. One of the reasons why it can be so addictive is the thrill or buzz it can provide. There is also the escape that gambling can bring from the problems and pressures of everyday life. Another lure is the feeling that the money is there to be won back, and so the problem gambler keeps trying to beat the system.

In the tick list below, tick which applies to you and your situation.

 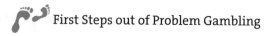

Problem gambler	Social gambler
I spend more than I can afford.	I keep within my financial constraints.
I am secretive about my gambling.	I use gambling as a form of entertainment.
I use gambling to cope with other stresses/problems.	I can take it or leave it.
I spend large amounts of money on gambling.	I have a limit to the amount I spend and stop when I have reached this.
I have the urge to gamble regularly.	When I feel down or stressed, it does not occur to me to gamble.
My relationships and/ or employment have been affected by gambling.	My relationships have not been affected by gambling.

The number of statements you have ticked on either side of the chart gives an indication as to whether you are more of a problem gambler or social gambler.

Problem gambling can affect a person's whole life, and it is often not just about excitement and entertainment. It can start off this way, but gambling can become a damaging activity that leads to feelings of helplessness and lack of control. This book is for those who are finding that gambling is affecting relationships or their work life, harming their own mental or physical health, or simply leading them into debt.

Problem gamblers are not all the same. People with gambling problems do not fit a stereotype and they come from all walks of life. Some develop gambling problems gradually over time, and others find themselves quickly spiralling into a gambling problem. Whichever it is for you, you are not alone.

Personal story
Mike, aged 40

Mike is a successful businessman with a large family. He has always enjoyed poker at his local pub. But, as a result of stress at work, he has become addicted to gambling. He is spending more and more time and money and using gambling as a way of escaping. He has recently come to the realization that he is a problem gambler because he is unable to stop and his relationships are suffering.

Personal story
Alice, aged 35

Alice lives in a racing town and enjoys a day out with her friends at the races. She does not gamble at any other time and simply looks forward to gambling as a social occasion. Alice is a social gambler, and, at this point in time, this is not a problem for her.

 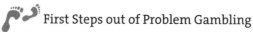

What are your reasons for gambling?

If you are wondering whether you are a problem gambler, you could ask yourself why you are gambling. Is it to win back money you've lost? Are you hoping for a big win? Do you gamble to escape life's problems? Do you enjoy the excitement of taking risks? Are you trying to feel better about yourself? Do you gamble to help cope with anxiety and depression?

The consequences of problem gambling

Problem gambling can have massive consequences, and for some people it can lead to a twenty-four-hour-a-day obsession. It can lead to problems such as:

- isolation
- damage to important relationships
- spending all one's time and money on this one activity
- borrowing from friends and family
- theft and debt
- lying to account for missing money and the need for more money
- difficulties at work or with studying
- psychological, emotional, and physical difficulties
- loss of employment
- low self-esteem
- using other means to deal with the strain of the debts, such as alcohol abuse, smoking, or addictive behaviours.

Problem gamblers may find themselves in a spiral of destructive behaviour. Statistics from GamCare callers indicate high levels of anxiety and stress among gamblers (40 per cent of the netline callers). For some, gambling can lead to breakdown in relationships and poor mental health.

The most obvious negative consequence of having a gambling problem is debt. Fifteen per cent of clients accessing help through GamCare were severely in debt and 42 per cent were facing more moderate levels of debt. The gambling industry in the UK is huge. According to government statistics, gambling has a turnover of £84 billion, making companies massive profits. Fifty per cent of callers to GamCare reported debts of between £6,000 and £50,000. When people addressed their gambling problem, their finances improved significantly. According to the GamCare Report of 2005, 83 per cent of clients presenting with debt had resolved their financial problems and there were none still in severe debt.

Maybe the goal of giving up gambling seems immense right now, but take a moment to consider the analogy of climbing a mountain. Looking up at the top when you are part of the way up can make you feel overwhelmed. However, if you take time to look behind you, back at where you have come from, you will notice that you have come some distance to get where you are now. In reality this means that you have used skills before in previous changes you have made, either in gambling or other areas, that have been successful – for example, when you have made small positive decisions to eat more healthily or go to bed earlier when you are tired.

Over to you!

Take a minute now to think about a small change you have made. How did you accomplish it and how did your life benefit? What skills did you use in making this change? Recognize that you already possess the necessary skills to have made progress in other areas.

There have been times, however brief, when you have managed to *not* have your gambling problem. It might have been for the sake of other people in your life or a decision made solely for yourself. Try to remember a time you managed this.

For example, when long-term gambler Ryan's relationship was in jeopardy, he managed to abstain for a two-month period. This showed Ryan that when he was in danger of losing something he really valued, he could demonstrate more self-control. It is likely that you will be able to recall similar small examples of success.

Exercise

Write down these successes that you have experienced, however trivial they seem.

_____

_____

_____

_____

What would your life look like without gambling? What would be different? For example:

- I would have more money to take my children out on a Saturday.
- My father would not keep asking me where all my money goes in his "suspicious voice", as if he knows I'm lying.
- I would feel happier and more sure of myself.
- I would feel that my partner trusts me.
- I would not waste whole evenings in front of the computer, but have time to ring friends and socialize.
- I would not have to lie to my mum about money or time I've spent out of the house.
- I would feel that *I'm* in control and not being controlled by sheer impulses.
- I would not feel as desperately low as I sometimes have done after a gambling binge.
- I would stand taller and hold my head up high.

If you are able to get a clear picture of how your life will be better for making these changes, they are more likely to happen. Have a think about what those close to you will notice about you after you've made these changes. Think about how you would be spending your time and energy in this new life. When you think about these things, think very specifically – for example, "What would I be doing in the time I am usually gambling?"

Mythbuster

A person has to gamble every day to be a problem gambler.

A problem gambler may gamble frequently or infrequently. If someone's gambling is causing financial, emotional, psychological, mental, or legal problems for themselves or others, then they have a gambling problem.

2

Self-assessment

I got into betting on the horses in my early teens. My interest grew gradually through friends and family members being into it; my dad used to take me to the betting shop at the end of our road on a Saturday morning to put a small bet on and I gradually grew more and more interested.

I began to spend hours looking at the newspaper on a Saturday. It was just a way of passing the time. I used to get a lot of satisfaction from meticulously writing out all the horses' names and charting how they had performed recently, and I really enjoyed the whole process of working

out how much I could win, then handing over my coins and sitting down with my paper to watch the race. The anticipation leading up to the race was a good feeling and this, combined with the actual moments the horses began running, was an enjoyable weekly event for me. My heart would race fast, and as the horses were running, everything in me would be saying, "Yes, you're winning, he's going to make it." I could feel the camaraderie as I joined with the other locals in the betting shop. There were different shouts of joy and triumph, combined with the sighs of hopes being dashed all around me. Then I would breathe a sigh of relief once the process was over, exhilarated.

In my late teenage years, this regular betting began to take up more of my money. I had begun to have more money available to me through my job with the local council, and betting took up more of my time and my thoughts and energy. I tended to let other things in my life fall to the background a bit. So, for instance, I would make excuses to not spend time with my friends who didn't gamble. Time with my parents or my brothers and sisters didn't interest me, and I would dive into my bedroom straight from work or make excuses to go out to plan or make my next bet. I also had a slow realization that to be so obsessed with betting was not normal in other people's eyes, so I would try to hide it or lie about it and make up stories about where I had been when I had been at the betting shop.

As the years went by, probably by my mid-twenties, it was beginning to dawn on me that other people my age, whose circumstances were similar to mine, were able to achieve financial stability; people around me were buying their own houses and having nice cars and clothes. Instead, I was still living at my parents' house, I didn't have anything to show for my money, I always owed my parents and friends money, and I felt a bit shabby in comparison to how they appeared to be. Subconsciously I was probably aware that I had a problem, which I guess is the reason I felt the need to lie and cover my tracks so much, but I had never actually said out loud to another or even admitted to myself, "I do not have the willpower to stop gambling." However, my gambling habit began to affect my relationships in terrible ways. For example, girlfriends began sensing that I was lying to them about where I was, and then this lack of trust would lead to arguments.

Later, when I got married and I was in a situation of having to share my money with someone else, my wife would find it hard to trust me, as I lied to her a lot about missing money that I had gambled away, and this again would lead to destructive arguments. So the gambling began to affect other areas of my life too; debts increased and, on occasion, I would be absent from work so I could watch an important race.

Eventually, one day after a particularly bad argument with Melanie, my wife, about some missing money, I began thinking, "Why is it I hurt people so much and I can't seem to stop?" and I would feel disgusted at my lack of self-control and regret my behaviour. I realized that my gambling hobby was actually an "addiction". I knew this mainly because when I tried to exert some sort of control over it, it was impossible. I acknowledged that when I tried to reduce *the amount of times I gambled in a week, I couldn't, and when I had some money allocated for something else, I would find it impossible not to gamble it away. When it came to the crunch, it was very hard for me to be honest with myself and actually say to myself, "You have an addiction to gambling." I remember looking in the mirror in shock and thinking, "You are a gambling addict." There was also a sense of relief and release in my admission as well. I was able to stop lying to myself and stop downplaying its effects on my life. This also meant that I could invite other people, including Melanie, into my thoughts and feelings about it, and I was able to take the mask off and admit my struggles. This was a huge hurdle for me and a major step in the very beginning of my recovery.*

This book is for anyone whose story has any similarity to Dave's. It's written for you if you are finding it hard to control your desire to gamble, or if your gambling habit has played a part in bringing damage to any area of your life. If you, like Dave, are worried about your gambling behaviour, or if people close to you are saying that they are worried about it, then we would encourage you to journey through the sections in this book.

Read through the statements on the next page and see how many you can identify with. If you tick the statements that most match your current thinking, you will get an idea of the extent of your current problem and it will also help you gauge your motivation to change.

1. I think I might be ready to make a move towards changing something about my gambling behaviour.
2. At last I'm doing some work on my gambling – it feels good/daunting.
3. I have been successful at working on my gambling, but I'm not sure I can do it without help.
4. I am really working hard to change.
5. I have changed but I do not want to go back to where I was with my gambling; I am reading this book so I won't relapse.
6. I thought once I had decided and put a lot of effort into curbing my gambling I would be free of it completely, but I keep finding myself struggling with it.
7. I wish I had more ideas on how to solve my problem.
8. I hope that this book will have some good advice for me.
9. I'm actually doing something about changing, not just talking about it, which is what I normally do.
10. *Other people in my life are worried about my gambling habits*
11. *I have felt suicidal before in the aftermath of a period of gambling.*
12. *I have debts as a result of my gambling.*
13. *I have stolen to fund my gambling.*
14. *My gambling behaviour or the effects that it has on me leave me depressed, anxious, or unable to sleep at night.*
15. *Gambling affects my work life.*
16. *I feel depressed or down about gambling.*

 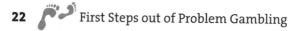

If one or more statements are ticked, read on! The more statements identified by italics, the more likely it is that gambling is a problem for you. However, if you ticked more statements in non-italic type, then you have already started working on your problem. You may have made good progress without even realizing it.

Mythbuster

Problem gamblers will take every opportunity to participate in any form of gambling.
Most problem gamblers have a favourite form of gambling that causes them problems and may have a secondary form of gambling that is not as problematic.

3

Building your motivation for change

Your level of motivation and incentive will determine the enthusiasm and effort you put into working towards change. Without sufficient and constant motivation, your endeavours to cease gambling will lose impetus.

This section will involve you in exercises that will enable you to:

- properly and realistically assess your current level of motivation to give up compulsive gambling;
- increase your level of motivation to such an intensity and consistency that it will carry you through the journey of changing your behaviour.

These exercises will help *you* to become the specialist in treating your problem of gambling. The concept of you being the person responsible for your change is essential if this self-help programme is to be successful and bring lasting success. This book will give you tips and techniques to put in practice, but only you can make the changes that are necessary to transform your life.

Over to you!

For these exercises to be a valuable tool in assessing and increasing your motivation, you will need to be prepared to:

1. Spend time every day doing them. Ideally, you should do them at the same time every day – for example, at the end of the day before settling down for the night or at another time when you feel comfortable and not hurried or rushed, and when you have time and inclination to be reflective. If it isn't obvious at first, try different times of day to find out what works for you.

2. Be honest with yourself about your own actions, thoughts, and feelings. This is sometimes hard – especially if it is an area which has brought about negative consequences and painful and difficult feelings. However, unless you are brutally honest with yourself when taking part in these activities, they will simply be lip service to the task of changing and will not properly aid you in tackling the major

issues that you need to in order to address the vast and complicated problem that gambling has become in your life.

Motivation is an important part of assessing change. If you look back to the statements that you ticked in Chapter 2, you will get an idea of the extent of your motivation to change.

One of the exercises designed to assess your motivation is to write down the pros and cons of gambling, as in the examples given below. Be sure you think of all the angles, dig deep, and think about all the aspects of your life.

Pros of gambling	Cons of gambling
I think I've been clever or skilful if I have a win, which makes me feel on top of the world.	Have felt very low when I've overspent. My partner and I fight all the time about this.
Win sometimes and get a good feeling when I spend the money of a win; it is like free money.	I feel like a rubbish parent and terribly guilty when I lose money that I could have spent on my children.
Gambling feels like a good "friend" at times.	I feel ashamed when I remember the lies I've told to cover my gambling secrets.

I have a role and good acquaintances in the poker world; we have a laugh.	I feel that gambling has control over me.
.	I get the feeling that my friends sometimes don't trust me with money.
Provides excitement.	Good feeling is temporary, leading to despair in the long term.
Takes away feeling of despair.	Massive debts.

Over to you!

How does this list make you feel? Are you more inclined to want to change after analysing the pros and cons?

Assess each pro and con on a scale of 1–10. Then turn to the next exercise, listing the pros and cons of giving up gambling.

Pros of giving up gambling	Cons of giving up gambling
Don't have to lie to my sister as to why I need money before payday.	I've become an expert at gambling now; it will all be a waste.
More money to spend on myself.	More time to fill.
More time to spend with my children.	Nothing to look forward to at the weekend.

Building your motivation for change

No shame when I look in the mirror.	May lose contact with my old racing friends, who've been part of my life for so long.
Opportunities for different social life could be more interesting.	Have to be inventive to find different ways to unwind at the end of the day.
No more deceit.	Less excitement and no escape from reality.

Now write a list of the things you have already lost through gambling. For example:
• Good credit rating; makes it hard for me to get a mortgage.
• Good feeling about myself.

Over to you!

What do you notice about what you have discovered in the "pros and cons" exercise? What is the difference between the nature/substance of the things on each list? It is common for people doing this exercise to realize that the things on the "pros of gambling" list are of short-term benefit – a good feeling or emotion – whereas the "pros of giving up" list usually includes more long-term and substantial things such as "develop good relationship with my partner", "gain more self-respect", "pay off debts". Therefore, the benefits of giving up gambling are far more valuable than the benefits of gambling. It is important to remind yourself of this and what you want to gain when you are battling with a craving or urge to gamble.

When I was about eight years old, my father took me to the races and let me put a small bet on. I can still remember the excitement and exhilarating feeling of waiting to see whether I had won. I begged him to let me go every week. I slowly started saving pocket money to spend on any kind of gambling and it became a part of my life. In my twenties, I had a job as a journalist and wrote about my gambling addiction, but far from being a cathartic experience, it became the only thing I could think about or write about after a while. I stole money from those nearest to me and destroyed friendships through not paying money back. I eventually gave up betting on horses, but only because betting shops started putting roulette machines on their premises and I became addicted to those. I continually denied having any kind of problem, ignored others, and hit rock bottom before I realized that I had to do something about my problem. I am slowly rebuilding my life.

Food for thought

It is not until you recognize and fully acknowledge the negative impact of your gambling that you will put efforts into stopping.

It is a certain "type" of person who is most susceptible to problem gambling.

Having a gambling addiction cuts across all age, economic, cultural, and class categories. There is no one type of person likely to become an "addict" or compulsive gambler. However, there are certain times in one's life when one is more likely to turn to gambling as a way of dealing with difficult emotions, such as the onset of retirement, the loss of a loved one, or being lonely. Often gambling starts out as a social activity, then slides into an addiction. For younger people it can sometimes be a result of peer pressure.

4

Setting your goal

The key question when preparing to make changes is: What is the ultimate goal? In addressing addiction and compulsive behaviour, you need to decide exactly what you are aiming towards. Think about the ultimate goal. Is it to stop gambling completely or do you simply want to reduce it through this self-help programme? We would suggest, however, because of the secretive and often "self-delusional" and "denial" nature of a gambling addiction, that abstinence is a more appropriate goal.

Food for thought
If you do not have a specific target to aim for, then you will not know whether you have been successful in reaching it.

Think about and write down your personal goal. For example, Dave realized that his goal was to be gambling-free and he decided to trust his family, as he came to the conclusion that he could not do it alone.

Revisit the self-assessment statements in Chapter 2. The more statements in italics that were identified, the more likely it is that you should consider abstinence. A short period of abstinence is valuable because if you see that you can be successful, even in the short term, this will provide something substantial. You are more likely to see change quickly, feel good about yourself and your self-control abilities, and even see other benefits – for example, more money in your pocket or a better atmosphere at home.

There is research that suggests that it takes thirty days to both make and break a habit. If you manage to have a period of abstinence for thirty days, you are likely to discover what works for you. There is a greater likelihood that you will lose the desire to gamble, and it is possible that you might be able to gamble recreationally in the future. Having said that, we would advise caution and suggest you do not rush into putting yourself into risky situations early in your recovery.

A temporary period of abstinence can also serve to break the habit. The longer you are away from associations connected with gambling, the higher the chance of ultimate success. The issue of associations and wrong or right choices will be explored in the next chapter.

Another way forward is to consider reduction. You need to measure how much you would usually spend in a gambling episode or in a "normal" week, and then set yourself a goal for reduction. It would also be a good idea to refer to the gambling diary, explained in Chapter 5, and reduce the number of times you gamble in a week. This would involve reducing to a level where your gambling is not a problem, or not as much of a problem, for yourself or others. This may be hard to work out at first, but unless you make a concerted effort to have a plan and set limits, you may find yourself spending more than you wish or even more than you realize.

Over to you!

Set a date to stop gambling. It is definitely a good idea to set a quit date. This is to allow yourself time to prepare. Your quit date should be an actual date. It should not be when your money runs out, or roughly a week before the next term at college starts, or next month. It is important to nail down the date and not change your mind about it. Sit down and think about a realistic quit date that you can and will stick to.

We recommend setting your quit date within one month of the current date. If you wait any longer, you are less likely to follow through. It is a great idea to set your quit date just before a holiday or other major event. Quitting gambling is a lifestyle change. If you attach it to another lifestyle change, you are more likely to be successful.

Most people can't quit because they don't know what to expect or don't have a plan. If you want to be fully prepared and successful when you stop gambling, you need a real, proper, written plan.

Sally had an online gambling habit and would put the children to bed and go online and play into the small hours. Her partner often worked away and she only realized her addiction when her partner questioned her about accumulated debts. After this, with the help of her partner, she devised a plan to abstain for months. She kept a gambling diary and developed a plan of other things she could do when her children went to bed. Looking back, Sally says that although she found it very hard, she reaped the benefits of complete abstinence, and the urge to gamble faded with time.

Mythbuster

Keeping a diary and writing down all my thoughts and feelings is simply an excuse for "navel gazing" and self-indulgence.

This is not true. Keeping a diary and writing down your thoughts and feelings will lead to you becoming more self-aware. Self-awareness is the key to discovering the good things about what you are already doing and the things you need to improve on.

5

Involving others

Tell someone close to you about embarking on this journey. Choose someone who you know wants the best for you and will not judge you. You need to know that they are good at listening and that you can be accountable to them. It will be so much easier if you are not feeling you have to go it alone, but that you have people to turn to when the going gets tough. Obviously, you need to choose your person wisely, remembering that your stuff is way too precious to share with everyone. Tell them about this book and discuss some of the ideas you encounter.

Something to think about

Many people mistakenly believe that to invite others into our hurts and struggles is weakness. In fact, the exact opposite is true. Our strength comes from our ability to share our journey with others.

People are not perfect, and it is often reassuring to others if you are able to share the less-than-perfect stuff with them. People have told us that often when they have begun to open up to others in this way, the other person feels that they too can open up about their own struggles.

The place of denial

As humans, we have a massive ability to lie to ourselves and pretend that everything is just fine when it's not. Denial is saying we are doing OK when we are not doing OK. Many gamblers have developed ways to avoid thinking about the true nature and extent of their behaviour. It may be that you recognize in yourself a tendency to deny to yourself and others the extent of your problem.

If this is the case, then facing yourself and facing up to the reality of bad choices will take courage. Walking out of denial can take effort, and part of this may be learning to be properly honest with yourself and others, especially the person you have chosen to open up to.

Congratulate yourself and celebrate your successes

When you have a success, however small or short-lived, don't forget to pat yourself on the back and remind yourself how far you've come. We are often good at berating ourselves for our faults, but slow to congratulate ourselves when we do well. It is a massive achievement to go for a period without gambling or to ride out a craving without succumbing to temptation, especially if we know that in the past we would have given in straight away.

It is a good idea to give yourself a small reward when you have reached a goal – you deserve it. However, make sure the reward is not gambling in any form – that would defeat the object! For example, when Sally, previously an online gambler, had reached four weeks of being gamble-free, she arranged a day out at a local spa with a friend to celebrate. Make sure you share your success stories with your well-chosen friend. Any friends you've invited to be on this journey with you will be pleased to hear that you've succeeded. Conquering an addiction is a massive achievement. Keep on saying "Well done" to yourself and keep going.

Whom do I tell?

If you're trying to change, there will be people who are really happy and supportive about the changes you're trying to make. But it is possible that others, without realizing it, may have a vested interest in you not changing. This may be a friend who also likes gambling and doesn't want to lose your company, or with whom you are "partners in addiction". You becoming a non-gambler may force them to face their own addiction. They may be jealous of your good progress. We are not saying that you can't be friends with them; just that you should be aware of the underlying reasons for potential conflict.

Can I see my gambling friends?
In the initial period, the places where you socialize may have to change, if those places are where you have previously gambled. Don't think of this as rejecting your friends, but simply as you placing yourself in a healthy environment for your recovery.

What about people who don't know I have an addiction?
We would advise caution and wisdom when choosing whom you tell about your addiction and recovery. Ask yourself what you would gain from disclosure and whether it would help you or hinder you on your journey. To judge for yourself whether you would be supported by them, it may help to ask yourself the following about the person in question:
• Would they want me to stop gambling?
• Do they want the best for me in my life?
• Do they have any vested interest in me staying addicted to gambling (e.g. the person who runs/owns the betting shop)?
• Will they judge me for having an addiction or secret?
• Will they be discreet about it or will it become common knowledge?
• Will it compromise my relationship with them and/or their ability to trust me (e.g. employers)?

Tell the truth or make an excuse

Sometimes we need to tell the truth about why we are not going to a certain place or taking part in a certain activity, and sometimes it is advisable to think of an alibi or an excuse to allow ourselves to avoid a risky situation. This will require careful planning and thought. Sam chose to disclose his addiction and his recovery to his manager at work when his team organized a work event at a local racecourse and he felt his good progress would be jeopardized. His boss was supportive and Sam was able to take himself out of a risky situation through his honest disclosure.

6

Ready, set, go!

Once you have assessed your own situation and built up motivation to change, it is time to prepare for making changes to your life. It is important that you prepare properly because this is key to your success. The exercises that you will be asked to do throughout this chapter will enable you to become much more self-aware. It is important to keep in mind the need for honesty and not allowing any place for denial.

In everyday life, many of our actions and reactions, including the ones associated with the habit of gambling, are automatic. They are behaviours that have become so much a part of who we are and our lifestyle that we are not conscious of the separate and specific thought processes behind them. If you drive a car or ride a bicycle, it is easy to see how this process of actions moving from the conscious into the automatic happens.

When you are learning to ride a bicycle or drive a car, a great deal of effort is required to remember, and put into practice, every thought process and action – for example, on a bicycle, trying to keep balance as well as turning the pedals and at the same time keeping the handlebars straight. In the beginning it requires effort and conscious thought. However, as these processes are repeated and practised, after a while they become automatic.

In the same way, your gambling actions are a learned and practised set of thought processes and are now almost unconscious reactions and actions. So, if you are able, by becoming more self-aware, to bring these thoughts and actions back from the unconscious, "natural", or automatic thing that you do into the conscious realm, you will recognize them afresh and be able to take steps to change and unlearn them. In time, self-awareness exercises and changing your actions, which will initially require a lot of thought and planning, will become automatic.

Exercise

Make a list of all the things that you do on a daily basis without being conscious of the mechanics of doing them. Break them down into components, finding out all the different stages and decisions you take automatically every day. For example:

- getting dressed
- brushing teeth
- making breakfast
- making sandwiches
- driving to work.

A man I know stopped driving to college for work because he realized that he had no memory of leaving his house, getting into the car, and driving until he arrived at his destination. The automatic nature of something he had done daily for years finally scared him because it was obsolete in his conscious mind. We all do things in this way and it is necessary to break down our actions to see what our thoughts, feelings, and behaviour actually are. We are, after all, responsible for all of these aspects of our existence.

Food for thought
If you have learned the habit of gambling, then you are able to unlearn it and learn a new way of reacting.

Impulses
In the next part of this chapter we will be introducing the gambling diary and discussing and looking more closely at our impulses to gamble.

Impulse; n. sudden strong urge to action. Tendency to act at once without deliberation. Thrust.

Roget's Dictionary

For our purposes here, an impulse is any desire, compulsion, or temptation you have to gamble. It may seem that you experience impulses randomly and for no reason whatsoever, but when you examine them you will find that a pattern emerges.

It is important that you make a daily list of your impulses for gambling so that you can recognize when, where, and who you are with when you feel the urge to gamble.

Alongside this, there are seemingly unimportant decisions you make in everyday life. You need to recognize these and be honest with yourself about small things which make an enormous difference in your life and, in effect, get you into situations which make gambling an option.

We experience impulses in different ways, for different lengths of time, and in varying degrees of severity and intensity. The level of impulse will be dependent on many different factors as diverse as:

• Day – payday or signing-on day.
• Time – lunchtime or walking home from work when you are alone and don't have to answer to anyone else for your actions.
• Emotion you are feeling/experiencing – stress.
• Person/people you are with.
• Sensual associations – prompts that you experience

 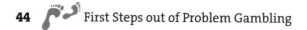

using one of the five physical senses (e.g. seeing a horse-racing advert on the television, seeing a slot machine, or hearing a conversation about gambling).

Exercise

Use the space below to identify the factors in your life which lead to you having an impulse to gamble. Think about last week and what specific factors led you to experience a greater desire to gamble on specific occasions.

_____

_____

_____

_____

Gambling diary

An important part of bringing your gambling behaviour from the unconscious into the conscious is recording your thoughts, feelings, and actions in an honest way. Find a notepad or journal and start a gambling diary, recording all of these things as they happen. Through recording them, you bring the behaviour into the open and can analyse the problem in its basic form. It gives you the opportunity to take a step back from your actions and look at them from a different perspective.

This honest recording is important because it takes away any vague nature of the intention to change. We all have notions of desiring to change many aspects of our lives, but seldom make any real progress in any of these areas. Dieters are a classic example of this. Many people feel that they want to lose weight and eat more healthily. They start a diet on Monday morning, but because they are not self-aware about their original eating habits, they are not in a position to consciously change them.

The subject of dieting provides an interesting comparison. There is research in which thirty participants began a diet with every intention of losing weight. Fifteen of the dieters also kept a food diary and wrote down everything they ate, and the other fifteen dieters didn't keep a food diary. At the end of the study period, the fifteen dieters who had religiously written down everything they had eaten had lost an average of seven pounds, whereas the fifteen who had not kept a written account of their food intake had failed to lose any weight and instead *put on* an average of seven pounds in weight.

This demonstrates what we all really know: humans are good at self-deception, and we can and do delude ourselves about our behaviour. The way to stop this is by determining to keep an honest and accurate account of our behaviour in relation to our gambling problem.

On the next page is a sheet for recording your gambling activities and thoughts. Have a look at it and see if you can fill it in. On the page after that is an example of one filled in, to give you an idea of how to make use of it.

Gambling diary

Date:
Day of the week:
Time:

Place where gambling impulse began:

How long impulse lasted:

Feelings and thoughts that make gambling more likely/feelings and thoughts during and after gambling took place:

Severity of the impulse to gamble (low, medium, high):

What happened? Did I gamble?
Yes, I did gamble.
Details – How much spent? Where did the money come from? How did I feel afterwards? What were my thoughts afterwards?

How much lost/won? Were there any repercussions for me or anyone else as a result of my choice to gamble?

No, I didn't gamble.
Details – How did I manage to not gamble as a result of this impulse? How did I feel? How long did the impulse last?

How did I feel after impulse had decreased or died down? Have I learned anything from this incident about myself or my ability to overcome impulses to gamble?

Gambling diary *(example of a completed sheet)*

Date:
30 October 2010

Day of the week:
Saturday

Time:
1.30 p.m.

Place where gambling impulse began:
At home watching TV. Flicked over to other side and caught ten minutes of horse-racing, which triggered desire to gamble.

Severity of the impulse to gamble:
Low

What happened? Did I gamble?
No.

Details:

Feelings: *Was relaxed at home on own before impulse began, slightly bored and at a loose end, so sort of knew if I was watching racing on TV, I was going to end up with desire to gamble.*

Thoughts: *If I go up to betting shop in town, that will sort me out for the afternoon, something to do; probably win something, which will give my day some excitement; will see a few friends in there too.*

 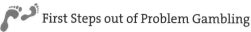

Versus a thought of: *Know that I don't want to spend any money today unnecessarily as I am skint at the moment. Also weighing up whether to go and get some money as haven't got any in the house, so I am definitely in two minds.*

It is important for you to complete your diary regularly, even when you do not actually succumb to your impulse to gamble but are tempted all the same. There is a blank copy at the back of the book. This way you can build up a realistic picture of your actual thoughts, feelings, and behaviour over time. Also, if you record the times when you manage to resist the impulse to gamble, you can identify and articulate those ways you overcame the temptation to gamble. Over time you can frequently make positive choices not to gamble by repeating what works for you personally, thus bringing about positive change for good.

Exercise

Practise filling out a gambling diary sheet about a time recently when you experienced an impulse to gamble. Be as honest and comprehensive as possible; the more you remember about what you do and record it, the more useful it will be as a tool for you to use. Get into the habit of doing this regularly.

Terry, aged 28

I know a big thing for me is that when I get bored or restless my mind starts wandering and I start thinking things like, "What horse is running today?" The more I think like that, the bigger and more intense the feeling that I want to gamble becomes, often until it almost overwhelms me and leaves me feeling that I have little choice other than to go down to the betting shop and put a bet on. Because I know and recognize this pattern of thinking and behaviour now, I have ready in my mind a list of things I consider doing when I first start to feel bored – stuff like watch a film, phone a mate and go for a drink, or go and see someone I can just pop in on – and generally this tactic works, and I now often manage to nip the urge to gamble in the bud before it develops into an overwhelming feeling that I find hard to fight against.

Food for thought

Remember that the more aware you are of your thoughts, feelings, and behaviour, the more likely you are to break the cycle of addiction.

Now that you've filled in the gambling diary and completed the various exercises, you'll probably find that you've got more of a handle on your addiction and your specific behaviour patterns. It is now time to look at the information you have gathered about yourself and put into practice some actions that others have used in reducing gambling.

Mythbuster

Some people never experience stress or bad emotions.

Everybody has good and bad things happen to them and, as a result, they experience negative emotions. However, someone who is emotionally mature has learned or developed ways of properly feeling the emotion that they are experiencing and then letting it go, or finding a way of "holding" it without it taking over their whole life.

7

Reducing gambling

Psychologists have developed an interesting theory as to how people change that breaks change down into different stages. People are all at different points in a process of change and these points are outlined below.

First of all, the person is unaware of any feelings of desire or need to change the way they act or think or both. They can stay in this state of (1) *precontemplation* their whole lives, or they can move on to a point at which they have a small inkling that they have a problem and wonder in a laid-back sort of way how they should deal with this. This stage is called (2) *contemplation*. Some people develop further into a place where they decide they are definitely going to change and make a plan of how they intend making that change. This place is the (3) *determination* or *decision* stage.

Once somebody has begun to take definite steps towards change and made some progress in operating their life in a different way, they are said to be in the (4) *action* stage of change. After taking action and making progress in changing their thoughts and behaviour, they move into the (5) *maintenance* stage. In this stage, the person is actively maintaining the changes that they have already made.

Exercise

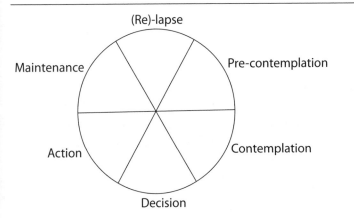

Cycle of Change

Where would you place yourself on this diagram of change? It may help to refer back to the statements you ticked on page 22. Have a go at trying to identify the stage you think you are at currently and whether you have changed at all recently.

Blips

During any of the stages of change, it is common for someone to experience a blip in progress, which can be identified as a lapse or even a relapse. A lapse is a shorter, more temporary step backwards in your progress in addressing your addiction. A relapse is a step back that lasts longer and becomes more serious and begins to pose a real threat to your progress. Each time you relapse it is possible to learn something from it that will enable you to progress further the next time you get back to the action stage of change. We revisit this in Chapter 8.

We revisit this in Chapter 8.

Personal story – Can you identify with my situation?

George, aged 40

I don't gamble every day, but I visit the big casino in Bristol about once a month, and it's a social thing with the boys. They all seem to be able to manage to spend a reasonable amount in the evening. But me – when I get there, I find it hard to put a lid on the amount I will spend. I'll go out with good intentions, but there will always be a point in the evening when I make the decision to go and get some more money; this inevitably leads to all the money being spent and then arguments in the morning when I've eaten into the overdraft to fund it. It is only recently that I have come to realize that it is an addiction. For me, I can't control it; when I'm there, the compulsion controls me.

If you have made it this far, you will probably have made it to the *contemplation*, *decision*, or even the *action* stage. The next section focuses on techniques for resisting or reducing the impulse to gamble. There is a short exercise after each technique.

Techniques for resisting/reducing impulses to gamble

Distraction

(a) Identify your feelings and your thoughts – for example, "I am feeling stressed, lonely, and looking for the next buzz."

(b) Combat the feelings or divert attention away from them by taking action that will alter those feelings – for example, watch a film, phone a friend or family member, have a conversation about something else, take a walk, cook a meal. You are the expert on yourself and what will work for you.

Exercise

Think of distraction activities that will really work next time you are experiencing an impulse to gamble.

Because, for me, the buzz from having a bet is so physically satisfying, often it helps if the alternative activity to distract me from gambling is physical too, so I will often try to quickly arrange a game of tennis or squash. In a way, it acts as a release of tension and stress or energy as well.

Reminding yourself of your long-term goals

Think and remind yourself of your long-term goals – for example, a stronger and better relationship with your partner as a result of greater trust because you no longer gamble, or being out of debt – and keep reminding yourself that the long-term goals will bring greater and longer-lasting satisfaction than the momentary pleasure that a gamble will bring.

Exercise

Write down what your own personal long-term goals are.

Changing your inner dialogue

We all speak to ourselves in our heads – through our thoughts most of the time – like a constant monologue, and these thoughts are either:

• negative – propelling us to negative moods or behaviour

- positive – propelling us towards positive moods or behaviour
- neutral or analytical – merely inner dialogue which observes or analyzes our surroundings and registers it.

For the purpose of changing our behaviour for the better, it is crucial that we identify those tendencies of ours that use negative thoughts and inner dialogue to change our mood or behaviour to negative, or which justify negative behaviour that we are planning or have acted upon already. Examples of this type of negative thought include:

- "It's only £5."
- "It's money I would have spent anyway."
- "I deserve this after the day I've had."
- "This will be the last time."
- "I just need this win."
- "Sod it."
- "This will teach her."
- "I'll start being self-controlled on Monday/next week."

Exercise

You can probably see in this list the sort of thing that you say to yourself and are now aware of plenty more that you use regularly. Write down the things you have as part of your personal negative inner dialogue. You may need to think about specific times and situations in your life to recall the exact type of thing you say to yourself.

Introducing positives

Now that you have identified your negative thoughts, we can move on to working out ways of consciously changing that tendency to excuse, justify, and move towards negative behaviour through your thought life. The way to do this is to remind yourself of your long-term goal of giving up gambling completely and the reasons why you want to do that, and then change the inner dialogue you have from negative thought patterns to positive thought patterns. By counteracting each identified negative thought with a positive thought, you can break or neutralize the effects on your behaviour. Eventually, this action of substituting positive inner talk for negative inner talk will become a good habit. For example, if prior to gambling you have the negative thought "It's only £5" and this justifies your actions of gambling, then you need to remind yourself of your long-term goal of stopping by using an appropriate positive thought instead – for example, "I don't need to gamble – I can do something else" or "I will use this money for something else; spend it on something that lasts and doesn't bring me down".

Exercise

Go through the list of negative thoughts above and the ones you personally use, then write down counteractive positive thoughts you could substitute when the tendency for negative inner dialogue kicks in. Practise replacing negative inner dialogue with positive inner dialogue.

Janet, aged 37

I've come to realize that my pride is a big hurdle I need to be constantly aware of. I find that if I get into a small amount of debt because of a gambling loss, then it will be my pride that whispers in my ear, "Don't worry – you can win it back," and this is pride that doesn't like me to admit my failings to my family or to myself and fails to recognize that I cannot win the money back through my own skill at gambling. The earlier I admit to myself that I have failed, the less likely I am to dig myself into a deep hole in terms of my gambling behaviour.

Riding out the impulse to gamble or to set yourself up

Impulses to gamble do subside. They definitely do decrease in intensity over a period of time. So, for example, a craving to gamble that occurs as a result of walking past a betting shop may be a strong impulse and may stay fairly strong for twenty minutes until you have arrived home. It is almost as if this period of time is the "danger zone", but you know that if you can ride it out until the end of the strong craving – out of the "danger zone" – then it will decrease in strength.

There are also the times when you kid yourself that you are doing something random – "just because" – but really you are setting the scene for you to gamble later on. Peter thinks and says to himself, "I will just pop to the shops to get a magazine," but, in the back of his mind somewhere, he is already aware that he can and probably will buy a scratch card at the same time. By making that first decision, he is setting the sequence of events and his inner dialogue in such a way that it becomes easier to fail later on. Dieters follow similar patterns. Maggie knows she wants to lose weight and eat healthily, but when she goes shopping she sees chocolate biscuits on offer and says to herself, "I'll just buy these for the kids," but really she has unwittingly paved the way for her to sabotage her own good efforts later on.

Exercise

Identify times in the last week when you have made any of these self-deceptive choices. Rack your brain and be honest with yourself.

Being aware of your emotions
Gambling can be used as a way of meeting our emotional needs. After you have identified some self-

deceptive choices you've made, next identify what emotion or feeling you were trying to change or escape from at that particular time and then go on to fill out the missing gaps.

When I feel

....

I want to gamble.

For example: tired, lonely, stressed, bored, unconnected to people.

When I have

....

I feel a desire to gamble.

For example: an argument with my partner; an evening to myself with no plans.

Now have a brainstorm, writing down everything you could possibly do instead in these situations. Be creative and use your imagination, then fill in the spaces below, replacing the word "gamble" with your new intended reaction. Speak these new intended reactions out loud throughout the next few hours in an attempt to reprogramme your brain. Remember that what you say out loud is very powerful.

When I feel
[as described above]
I want/I will choose to

....

For example: phone a family member; have a cup of tea; tidy up; pop a sweet into my mouth.

When I have [as described above] I will choose to

For example: go for a walk; read a magazine; cook a meal.

....

Being aware of wrong thinking

One of the main types of wrong thinking that leads to habitual gambling is distorting reality. This means either exaggerating or underplaying the importance of an event. There are many different ways we do this. For instance, you may think or say, "I know that I've not gambled in the last week, but it's only because I haven't had time." Here you are minimizing your current achievement, which isn't very good for your feeling of self-worth; if you have done well, it is important to acknowledge it.

Another common example of distorting reality is: "It was only a tenner I lost; I usually win anyway." This is both minimizing the loss and magnifying the gain, thus propelling yourself to further gambling.

Over to you!

Read your body's signs of getting stressed! It is helpful to be aware of the physical signs that you are getting stressed because it is more likely that you will give in to temptation to gamble if you are caught unawares. If you can spot the signs, then you are more likely to make moves towards dealing with stress in a good way.

Remember a time recently when you became stressed and/or overwrought emotionally. Do you remember any of the following occurring?
- Heart beating faster
- Sighing
- Tightness in the head
- Headache
- Shaking
- Tension in the neck
- Butterflies in the tummy.

Mythbuster

Most other people feel good about themselves 100 per cent of the time.
Everybody has days and times when they are more aware of their failings. And most people, in order to feel good about themselves more of the time, have to work at it. This entails recognizing their strengths, working to increase them, and reminding themselves of these regularly.

8

Avoiding relapse

Gambling is widespread, legal, and socially acceptable, especially with the rise of internet gambling. It can feel as if there are opportunities to gamble everywhere. This can make it difficult for former gamblers to stay on the straight and narrow.

Alternatives

Now that you are well on your way on your recovery journey, it is a good idea to think of ways to maintain your progress and prevent falling back into old ways. You need to remind yourself of what you are going to say to certain people, as outlined in Chapter 5, when they ask you about gambling.

In this period, when your efforts are concentrated on avoiding relapse of any sort, you need to realize that at some point someone is likely to invite you to engage in a gambling activity, and you need to consider your reaction in advance. One recovering gambler, Phil, decided to say to his old gambling friends, "I don't do that any more; it was costing me too much money. But we can do this instead…" He was being honest but firm, as well as providing himself and his friends with an alternative. Try to think of alternative activities to suggest if faced with the situation of a friend inviting you to gamble.

Access to money

Think about your access to money: how you can get it and what barriers you can put in the way of getting it and giving in to temptation. Think about how you have paid for gambling in the past and put these means out of your reach. This may take effort and you may need to swallow your pride and ask another person for their help in this. For example, Kathy decided that until she felt stronger, she would give her credit card, which she would have used for online poker, to her sister to look after.

One day it'll creep up on you: you'll find yourself in a place where temptation presents itself. It may be a pub with a slot machine or something else that you find hard to resist. You will need an action plan to manage this risky situation. You could rehearse in your mind what you will do and say in these situations. For example, Tim went for a drink with his wife. She went outside to speak on her mobile phone, and he was left facing the temptation of a gambling machine nearby, its flashing lights inviting him to play. He managed this situation by taking action: he found a newspaper, which kept him occupied until his wife's return. It may be worth taking a form of distraction out with you if you recognize that a gambling temptation may be nearby.

Exercise

With the above example of Tim in mind, it would be a useful exercise to record your behaviour when avoiding temptation. Write down the thoughts and feelings that you experienced your own situation when you've been tempted recently:
What happened? ....
My thoughts were: ....
My feelings were: ....
My behaviour was: ....
What do you notice? What can you learn? What can you take with you into your next temptation-laden experience? ....

Avoiding old haunts

There will be old places/lifestyle routines that you will recognize as part of your gambling repertoire. If you continue to go to those places or engage in those routines, you will eventually give in to the temptation to gamble. You need to find positive new places or adopt new routines, so that you are not leaving an empty space or gaps where gambling has been. Jane, a long-term gambler in recovery, stopped going to the betting shop on a Friday lunchtime and made sure that she arranged to meet a friend for coffee instead. She consciously took herself out of temptation's way and filled the gap with an enjoyable activity.

If your particular place of gambling is more accessible – the internet, for example – then you need to be creative in avoiding this. Jenny had an online gambling problem and knew that if she came home after a night out and saw her laptop downstairs, she'd be likely to log on and, before she knew it, would be in the grip of gambling. Once she recognized this, she made a plan. Before a night out, she asked if she could put her laptop in her housemate's room. This took preparation, planning, and creative thought, as well as being honest and accountable to her housemate.

For you and your specific problem area, you will need to sit down and properly consider how you will avoid potential gambling situations. Write down situations and your potential solutions.

The danger of swapping one addiction for another
What some people find on this journey – where they have begun to see some success in conquering this problem behaviour, and where they have managed to go some time without gambling or reduce their gambling quite significantly – is that they can get

addicted to something else almost unconsciously. It is easy to see how this happens. For example, instead of going to the betting shop on days off, someone starts to spend his days off in the pub with a friend. However, quite without realizing it, he has managed to become a heavy drinker, as one addiction is replaced by another.

To avoid this, you need to remain extra vigilant after the initial hard work of beginning to make good changes. These new habits can happen slowly and subtly, like a landscape eroding over time. If you think this has begun to happen to you in any area, you need to pinpoint the problem and take action very quickly. You need to build up the land that has slipped. Do this by using the skills and techniques you have learned through this book, also remembering to be accountable to the friend sharing your journey.

Self-esteem

When you are confronting a gambling habit, it is highly possible that you are suffering from low self-esteem, as most people do at some stage in their lives. This could be one of the factors that helped lead you into your compulsive behaviour and habits, or the lifestyle resulting from your gambling could have decreased your self-esteem.

People who suffer with low self-esteem often think negative things about themselves. These could include statements such as "I'm worthless", "I hate myself", "There is nothing nice about me", "I'm so unpopular/

fat/ugly", or "No one likes me". These negative statements can run over and over in your mind, especially when things are not going well for you, and they can lead to a depressing downward spiral of negative mood and thinking. If you can relate to this, you are not alone. This is a very common problem. Identify the sorts of negative things that your thoughts default to on a bad day:

_____

_____

_____

_____

_____

To combat this, you need to take a careful look at yourself and search for the good things about you that are true and real. These can be skills, abilities, good ways in which you may relate to others – the sort of thing someone who knows and likes you might think about you. Identify at least five positive personal qualities you have:

_____

_____

_____

_____

_____

Rules

If we suffer from low self-esteem, we sometimes have a tendency to develop rules in our head as to how to cope with everyday life. So someone may say to themselves, "If I manage to go the whole week without gambling, then I'm OK/I'm a good person." Another person may have rules about eating healthily for the day and then think, "If I fail, then I am a real hopeless case." So rules may appear to be a good thing, but if we fail – which we might do – this feeling that we have broken the rules may lead to low self-esteem and feelings of hopelessness. Rules that we impose upon ourselves are sometimes good, but we must be able to identify those rules to make sure they are helpful to our progress and not use them as another stick to beat ourselves with if we fail.

Identify rules that you live by (these may relate to gambling or other areas of your life):

_____

_____

_____

_____

_____

Taking stock exercise

Now would be a good time to take stock of where you are right now on your journey. On a scale of 0–10 (0 being the very worst you could be, and 10 being the very best you could be), where would you place yourself now?

Terry, a recovering gambler, said he was a 4 in this exercise. He was able to identify the positives about where he was now. So he was able to say, "I'm not a 2 or a 3 because I have gained a measure of self-control over my gambling." He was also able to identify where he wanted to be. He saw that if he could reduce gambling a little more, he would achieve his goal of being an 8 on the scale.

Have a go yourself at thinking about how your life would look if you reached a little higher on the scale. (This scale idea is one expounded by an organization called Brief and is part of a therapy called Solution Focused Therapy. You can read more about this on their website www.brief.org.uk.)

9

What if I slip?

However far up the ladder of recovery you go, it is possible that relapses will occur during recovery. Relapse is not inevitable. Some people never gamble again after starting recovery. But many others relapse, once, twice, or many times.

If you find yourself in a state of relapse, don't worry; be encouraged that you can use this as a learning incident. A relapse never "just happens"; it is a diversion, a mini deviation from your recovery journey. This deviation has resulted in you making the choice to gamble. The choice to gamble was not the first thing to happen; it was the outcome.

So, to discover why you have relapsed and made the decision to gamble on this occasion, you need to retrace your steps. You need to work backwards to recognize what led you to relapse. It is very common to slip and it's really important to give yourself a break.

Think about it

What has led you to relapse? Identify irrational thoughts or feelings. Have you reacted to urges, impulsive behaviours, or triggers?

If you have slipped in your endeavour to be gambling-free, then it's a good idea to revisit the "pros and cons" exercise in Chapter 3 to remind yourself of why you began this journey. OK, maybe you have begun to slip, but you can simply say to yourself, "Stop – don't slip any further." You don't have to wait until Monday or until you've lost all your money or won back what you've lost. You are free to stop this blip right this second. Take control of the situation.

Many people think to themselves, "I've blown it. I might as well go and blow it properly." They are in a "sod it" mentality and feel like throwing in the towel. If this is how you're feeling, resist the temptation to slip even further. Tell your positive friend about your slip and keep on being accountable to them. Make a proper plan for the next few weeks and be specific about the times and situations you find hard.

It might be that you are feeling fearful – afraid that it's all going wrong, that success is out of your grasp, and that you are losing control.

You are in control now. You have a choice: either you let the fear control you and how you react to your slip, or you realize that you have the power to overcome it. Stop thinking about the big weight of conquering a whole addiction. Sit down, get your microscope out, and look in detail at your life, step by step.

Recap

Recap on the times you've recognized seemingly unimportant decisions (see Chapter 6) and where you have avoided temptation. There will be some positives, even if you have slipped. Maybe you haven't met with old friends that you used to gamble with. Recognize how far you've come.

Recovery is like building a house. You don't have to start from scratch now – you've already laid a foundation with all your preparation, and every day that you are successful is like another brick in the building.

Remind yourself of the cycle of change that we looked at in Chapter 7 and see where you would place yourself now; you will probably be surprised that you are certainly further on than when you began this journey.

Stress and its antidote – relaxation

A big reason why people relapse is stress. Some people cope with stress better than others. Stress is part and parcel of existence and we need to find effective ways of coping with the natural stress in our lives.

Often people dealing with addictions recognize that they have used their addiction as a place of refuge and safety from the stresses and strains of life, and report that they find it hard to incorporate relaxing into their

 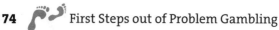

daily life. Knowing how to relax is a skill we can learn. Relaxing is not just sleeping or doing nothing, although it can be. Relaxation is about ushering calmness and peace into our lives. This means ensuring that your lifestyle is more peaceful – on lots of different levels. It can mean turning the television off, having less background noise, eating healthily, not allowing yourself to get over-tired, doing things you enjoy, spending time with people you like and who make you feel good. Relaxation can also be used very specifically as an antidote to the ills of stress, pressure, and anxiety: it can be used to target negative emotions.

Think about it

By relaxing, you are acknowledging your value, that you are important, that your emotional well-being is important, and that you need to care for yourself.

Stress is a part of modern daily life, but it is often a trigger for a person to seek release through indulging in their addictive behaviour – a sort of self-comfort idea. It is crucial to find ways to lessen the stress in your life and to identify effective ways to unwind daily. Rather than simply spending an evening in front of the TV, it would be worth trying, actively and consciously, to relax in different ways. Here is a short relaxation exercise for you to use.

Relaxation exercise

• Find a quiet place where you will not be disturbed. Sit with your eyes closed, legs outstretched, and let your arms hang down to your sides. Consciously empty your mind of all worries, thoughts, and images. Visualize a blank screen.

- Say slowly out loud to yourself, leaving space in between each phrase to experience the effect of relaxation:

  "Quiet and soothe my mind."

  "Relax my mind."

  "Rest and relax my body."

- Next, concentrate on slowly stretching and then relaxing every part of your body in turn from your neck, including arms and hands, right down to your toes.

- Now consciously decide to let go of any bad feelings of resentment, hurt, pain, or anger you may have experienced today or this week, saying, "I choose to let go of you," and naming the negative emotion (e.g. anger, sorrow) as you exhale.

- Finally, say to yourself, "Completely be refreshed and soothed, my soul."

How do you feel now? Was this a useful exercise? If it was, then we suggest that you make time for this every day to maintain a healthy stress level. If it wasn't a relaxing experience, then it is worth trying meditations on DVDs or other relaxation techniques. You need to find out what works for you, as it's very important to know how to achieve relaxation and fit it into your life.

10
Moving forward

This book is a self-help book and we are not asking you to delve into your psychological history, although if you feel that doing so would be useful, we suggest you access professional help to examine some of the sources of your addictive behaviour.

It can be helpful, however, to list all the stresses in your life, everyday things that may cause you to feel anxiety or rage, which you relieve through gambling. It is amazing how long the list can be.

Also, think about the source of addiction in terms of unresolved issues, childhood traumas, and what this behaviour of gambling is seeking to hide or displace. We really recommend counselling for any unresolved childhood issues that are still causing you pain or unwelcome feelings. In particular, any experience of abuse, bullying, trauma, or parental neglect will need to be explored.

I have struggled to varying degrees with a gambling addiction since my late teens, and I now attend a local church and they have a support group specifically for people who struggle with addictions. I go there one evening every week; I'm the only one who has a gambling addiction – mostly, the others struggle with alcohol addictions – but the thing I find really helpful is the sense of accountability that I feel to the other members. Although we all struggle with similar temptations and downfalls, I know that I cannot pull the wool over their eyes as I feel I can with other people in my life. On a regular basis they ask tough questions and don't let me get away with vague or pat answers. The atmosphere in the group is honest, open, and non-judgmental.

Through this group I have a mentor, who has gone through similar experiences and whom I can ring at any time when I'm struggling, and he encourages me and allows me space to talk through what I'm feeling. I have been on my journey out of a gambling addiction for four years and so far have managed to stay "gamble-free" for this time, with two fairly short-lived relapses. I feel a greater sense of peace, am more in control of my urges and behaviour, and I no longer feel shame.

I would say to anyone with a gambling problem to get people in your life like this, either an organized group – Gamblers Anonymous, a church or community support group – or simply someone a little bit out of your immediate home situation who is not closely affected by your gambling, whom you can ask to be accountable to. There are also websites that you can go on, which I have found have helped me. I find that I can blog, which is good because if you try and give up and choose not to gamble any more, you can bet your life that you will still think about it all the time, and you can vent through a blog or a diary or a journal.

The "lifetime" exercise

To help you further with this, reflect on your life and also reflect on your journey out of addiction so far. We call this a "lifetime" exercise. Number the points on a line, starting from zero, to represent the years of your life so far. First, mark on the line the significant events that have happened in your life, both good and bad. After this go back and mark in when you first started gambling, and how and why. Consider issues such as whether the nature of the gambling has changed at any point, when it first started to become an addiction, and how it related to the positive and negative events you have already marked. It may be useful to do this exercise with the help of a close friend or family member to prompt you.

Example: Mike's lifetime highs and lows

Years

0

1   Mum and Dad married.

2   Sister born.

3

4

5

6   Mum and Dad out a lot; had a lot of babysitters.

7

8   Grandma died.

9

10

11   Started middle school.

12

13

14   First started playing gambling games.

15   First sexual experience.

16   Left school; got first job; left home; lived in flat with mate.

17   Boring jobs; gambled at lunchtime to relieve boredom and get some excitement in life; probably when addiction started. Most friends liked to have a flutter; people saw me as the one into the horses big time.

18   Back to college; not earning so much; got into debt; still gambling a lot; no one to answer to.

19

20

21

22

23

24 Met partner; gambling caused lots of arguments
from the beginning.

25 New job.

26 First child born; greater motivation to not gamble;
started attending Gamblers Anonymous.

27 Had to sell car to pay off big debt as a result
of gambling.

28 Bankrupt.

29

30 Second child born.

31 Had to remortgage house due to increasing debt.

Making amends

As part of your recovery, it is essential that you are
willing to admit the times in your life when you
have hurt people. Make a list of those people. If it is
possible for you to make amends to some or all of those
people, then do so in whatever way is appropriate –
for example, saying sorry to a partner, ex-partner, or
friend, and acknowledging the pain that has been
caused. If the person you have hurt, even if you did so
unwittingly, is no longer around, it might be helpful for
you to offload any guilt you have been carrying around
onto someone else whom you are able to speak to about
this situation, or even to write down how you feel
about the things you have done to hurt others.

Jackie, aged 60

As a result of my addiction and other character weaknesses, I did something awful to my sister. When my dad died, I was left in charge of distributing the money from the will and I stole a large chunk of the money to support my habit and gave her a minimum amount. She had no knowledge of my deception, but it was a huge weight on my mind. As part of my recovery, I was encouraged to make amends in this relationship, so I plucked up the courage to tell her. When I did, it was an amazing release, knowing that she knew, and I was lucky enough that she did not seek revenge or even ask for the money back. Knowing that I have faced my demons is really significant and I feel tons better in having an honest, shame-free relationship with my sister.

Rachel, aged 28

Because much of my coping with the lifestyle that my gambling addiction has led me into is shrouded in lies, cover-ups, and deceit, I feel that I need to really try and remain "secret-free". So, to that end, I have endeavoured to make sure I have told one person every single thing that I have ever done or felt shame about, and in doing this I feel that my previous secrets have no hold or power over me as they are now in the open. And if my mind wanders into feelings or thoughts of guilt or embarrassment about the

past, I can say to myself with certainty, "I have dealt with that; it is no longer unfinished business."

Here I was again… another crisis where I'd spent money that I couldn't afford to lose, money put into an account for our family holiday. I was in another situation that had only been brought about by my gambling habit.

I'd often been told by my family and friends that I gambled too much and that gambling made me difficult to trust, difficult to live with. However, it wasn't until I reached the end of myself, until the stress of holding myself together in another self-made financial and emotional crisis was too much to bear – when I felt absolutely rubbish about myself – that I decided to begin to make the changes needed to break away from gambling.

In the wreck of my life, I felt unhappy, scared, and ashamed, and I plucked up the courage to ring my parents and tell them what had happened, and the full extent of my gambling problem. Then I had the massive task of being open with my partner. She was not happy but she tried hard not to make me feel any worse than I already did. She really did want me to make a change in my life and she wanted to support me in it. I started to seek out people to give me support online, and I poured out my heart to my friends and family, which wasn't at all easy.

Through my gambling diary, I began learning to become honest with myself and others around me, and in doing this I began to face things about myself. With great effort and determination, I weaned myself off gambling. Over time I have begun to experience and feel emotions that before I would have gambled away. My ultimate goal now is to reach the end of every day without having a gamble. I'm grateful that there is material and support out there. Six years have gone by and now today my family has a dad and partner who spends time with them. I have a sense of peace, and my good feelings about myself seem to be growing. I am trustworthy, even with money, and no longer feel tempted every day. I have stayed gamble-free and my life is very different now.

Over to you!

You are now in a position to have a story, like Joe's, of your journey so far. We would like you to look back at how far you have come and to recognize and celebrate your success. Write down your story, using the pointers below to direct you. It may take some time, and a lot of hard work and determination, to go back through the hard journey of your story.

The things that prompted me to start the journey towards change:

_____

_____

_____

Five times I have felt the pressure to gamble, but have avoided gambling:

1.
2.
3.
4.
5.

What I have learned about myself on the way:

_____

_____

_____

_____

The hardest things I have found are:

_____

_____

_____

_____

Five strengths/skills I possess, which will help me on my journey towards my goal:

1.
2.
3.
4.
5.

For the family

This chapter is for you if you have a friend or family member who is struggling or has struggled with a gambling addiction. We do not know your story, but we imagine that if you have shared your life in any way with someone who is a compulsive gambler, you will have experienced hurt, disappointment, frustration, and other negative emotions as a result of their behaviour. It is OK, and even healthy, to admit to yourself how much you've struggled with liking and accepting this person when what they have done has caused you great pain. This is not your fault; none of it is within your power to change. This is their journey and they are responsible for the way they have behaved and the mistakes they have made. Letting go of guilt, even false guilt, is very important, as it will better enable you to be a good support and help for them on their journey without causing an unnecessary burden.

Simon's son, who is twenty-nine, has struggled with a gambling problem for many years. The stress and anxiety of always worrying about what problems were going to come up were making Simon ill and unable to function normally. It was not until he decided to let go of his son emotionally, and say to himself that as much as he loved his son, he couldn't carry him, cover up for him, or even change him, that he was able to feel stronger emotionally.

Letting go... of them

Letting go of someone is not saying that you no longer love them or support them. In letting go, you are saying that *you* are important and *your* emotional well-being is of value. This may mean not bailing your loved one out when they rack up huge debts and making sure you protect yourself financially from gambling debts if at all possible.

Emotional fallout

To be a proper support, you need to be emotionally "healthy" yourself. In essence, this means spending time with others, apart from the compulsive gambler. At times the addiction can feel all-consuming and overwhelming.

Personal story

Ginnie, aged 30

Ginnie's husband was a gambler who spent lots of money in betting shops on horses. She had reached the point at which, every time he came in, she would go through his pockets, looking for evidence of gambling. Even when she didn't find anything, she would be wired and consumed by anxiety. It was a legitimate feeling, based on concrete evidence of the past experiences, that led to these panic episodes. However, the reality was that the anxiety and panic left Ginnie powerless and devastated. When Ginnie was able to recognize this and seek support, and help herself by asking

*her doctor, gaining support from friends, and going online
to meet other supporters, she began to feel more empowered
and less weighed down herself.*

Often someone with an addiction may have got
themselves into a pattern of behaviour that involves
deceit, lies, or covering up for misdemeanours. So
when they are in "recovery" and are trying to break
this negative pattern of behaviour, it may be that other
negative emotions surface which surprise you. These
might include anger, resentment, paranoia, blame,
shame, and hurt. Don't take these personally; they
should pass as recovery progresses. It may be that you
would benefit from outside support or help; counselling
is an option. Going to your doctor would be your first
step, and they would be able to recommend counselling
services locally. Some people find support from online
groups, religious groups, churches, or organizations
such as the Quakers or the Samaritans. More sources of
support are given in the *Useful resources* section at the
back of this book.

Getting outside help could mean that you don't feel
overwhelmed and over-burdened, and it can sometimes
give you a more objective view of the situation.

This journey is likely to be hard for the recovering
gambler and for you. There are online groups which
allow you to offload your fears, worries, and concerns,
and help you to feel less alone. Gam-Anon and
Parents of Young Gamblers can also offer support

and help. These organizations can provide a forum where you can speak to others who understand what you are going through and what it is like to support a recovering gambler.

Letting go... of the past

It is probable that the person who has been enslaved by a gambling addiction has hurt you and caused you problems. It is a good idea to see if you can let go of this past hurt and resentment and keep on wiping their slate clean, to keep your relationship with them good and positive. Forgiving them does not mean letting them get away with behaving badly, and it does not mean that the hurt was not real and not important; it just means you are choosing to let go of the hurt, anger, and pain of the past, so that it no longer affects you as severely. Counselling or speaking to someone else outside of your situation may help with this.

The power of encouragement

Your biggest gift to the person you are supporting is encouragement. We all need encouragement and to know that others believe we can be successful. We are not used to saying "Well done", especially in our culture. We fear sounding insincere or patronizing, but the person who is making changes and putting in lots of effort really needs to know that you have noticed those changes, however small they may seem.

Think about it

Listening and being available to listen is important. How can you show this person that you are there for them?

Throughout this "First Steps" book there have been exercises to complete, and it may be that you can ask the person you are supporting how they have found these. Ask if they've learned anything new, and engage them in conversation about what they are being made aware of. Remind them that you are there for them, even if it is a small thing such as a text. It can be so encouraging when you're having a hard day just to open a text message flashing on your phone from a friend saying, "Thinking of you"; it feels good to know that you matter to someone.

Share the things that *you* find hard in life. It may be that you've got a history of always being the one who provides support; perhaps to share something of your own struggles may mean that any power imbalance that exists is lessened.

Protect the other person appropriately, but don't overly shield them from the natural consequences of the addiction.

Change is gradual, so don't expect too much too soon. You need to be aware that they may relapse and that relapse is a common feature of addiction and recovery. If the person you are supporting does relapse, they are bound to feel very bad about this. So, despite your disappointment, it is worth remembering that they are still trying and your valuable support is still needed.

The issue of control

The person who is addicted to gambling often feels that they have little control over their addiction, themselves, and therefore their lives. Often people close to them, in trying to help them to limit the damage, will be tempted to take away what little control they do have.

Becki was gutted to find out that her husband owed a substantial amount of money; she then took control of all the finances. This worked, initially, in giving her a sense of safety and limiting the damage to the household finances. However, ultimately, this did not deal with the addiction; it also led to growing resentment for Dave, as their relationship became unequal and full of suspicion. They began to get round it by having honest and open dialogue about their feelings. They decided to come to a compromise, with him being given control over a small amount of money on a weekly basis. The meant he was to able to win back her trust and test out his newly learned strategies.

The dynamics of human relationships can become unequal, especially if one partner struggles with addiction, and it is important for the "supportive" one not to place themselves, inadvertently, in a "parental" role.

Useful resources

Suicide prevention

It is important that you have access to a 24/7 helpline for any time that you are feeling low, depressed, anxious, or even suicidal.

UK

Samaritans provides a confidential emotional support 24 hours a day. The telephone number for the UK is 08457 909090, or visit the website to find more information or your local branch.
www.samaritans.org

USA

National Suicide Prevention Lifeline
Toll-free 24 hour phone: 1-800-273-TALK
www.suicidepreventionlifeline.org

Canada
Centre for Suicide Prevention

Crisis Line

Different states have different helpline numbers. Find out the one for your local area on www.suidiceinfo.ca or telephone Crisis Line (24 hours a day) 613-722-6914/1-866-996-099
www.crisisline.ca

Counselling

For general or more specific counselling, contact your doctor for a list of talking therapy providers in your area.

UK – National Health Service

In different local areas the NHS provides different access to talking therapies. www.nhs.uk/livewell/counselling provides information on this and introductions to counselling articles and video.

 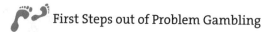

Gambling support

UK

Gam-Anon is the UK fellowship for those affected by compulsive gambling. Their meetings are for the friends and families who've been affected by a gambler. They offer tips and advice for family members about how to cope with a compulsive gambler and how to support them in their journey towards abstinence. Gam-Anon meetings are available in many areas; go online to check whether there are any in your area.
www.gamanon.org.uk

Gordon House Association (Residential and rehabilitation)
186 Mackenzie Road, Beckenham, Kent BR3 4SF
Telephone: 020 8778 3331 (13 bed unit)
Somerset Mews, 43/47 Maughan Street, Dudley, West Midlands DY1 2BA
Contact houses direct – ring for application form and more information.

GamCare (Units 2 and 3, Baden Place, London SE1 1YW) provide a phone line service 0845 6000 133 (8 a.m. to 2 a.m., seven days a week) to anyone who is gambling or is worried about someone they know. They can provide advice, emotional support, counselling, and online advice, including one-to-one support and advice for problem gamblers, their partners and family.
www.gamcare.org.uk

Parents of Young Gamblers provides advice and help and support for parents of young gamblers in the West Midlands.
Telephone: 0121 443 2609

Gamblers Anonymous is an organization through which people who are struggling or have overcome a gambling addiction join together in self-help groups in local areas and provide each other with support and accountability.
Helpline: 020 7384 3040
www.gamblersanonymous.org.uk

General addiction support

UK

Action on Addiction
– Gambling addiction is focused on (as well as other addictions) with lots of online information.
www.actionaddiction.org.uk

Canada

Centre for Addiction and Mental Health
Their website provides journals, articles about mental health and addictions, including gambling.
www.camh.net

Brief Solution Focused Therapy – Brief is an organization specializing in problem behaviour and trying to change it by looking at "solution behaviour", there is information on their website about how to use it in overcoming problems.
www.brief.org.uk

We have recommended counselling as a way to explore your past and other personal issues. A book that provides a taster and a light-hearted introduction is *Counselling for Toads: A Psychological Adventure* by Robert de Board (Routledge 1997).

Appendix

Gambling diary

Date:
Day of the week:
Time:

Place where gambling impulse began:

How long impulse lasted:

Feelings and thoughts that make gambling more likely/feelings and thoughts during and after gambling took place:

Severity of the impulse to gamble (low, medium, high):

What happened? Did I gamble?
Yes, I did gamble.
Details – How much spent? Where did the money come from? How did I feel afterwards? What were my thoughts afterwards?

How much lost/won? Were there any repercussions for me or anyone else as a result of my choice to gamble?

No, I didn't gamble.
Details – How did I manage to not gamble as a result of this impulse? How did I feel? How long did the impulse last?

How did I feel after impulse had decreased or died down? Have I learned anything from this incident about myself or my ability to overcome impulses to gamble?

Also currently available in the "First Steps" series:

First Steps out of Depression
Sue Atkinson

First Steps out of Eating Disorders
Dr Kate Middleton
and Jane Smith

First Steps out of Problem Drinking
John McMahon

First Steps out of Anxiety
Dr Kate Middleton

First Steps through Bereavement
Sue Mayfield